ELEGY

ELEGY

Poems by

MARY JO BANG

Graywolf Press

SAINT PAUL, MINNESOTA

Publication of this volume is made possible in part by a grant provided by the Minnesota State Arts Board, through an appropriation by the Minnesota State Legislature; a grant from the Wells Fargo Foundation Minnesota; and a grant from the National Endowment for the Arts, which believes that a great nation deserves great art. Significant support has also been provided by the Bush Foundation; Target; the McKnight Foundation; and other generous contributions from foundations, corporations, and individuals. To these organizations and individuals we offer our heartfelt thanks.

"Three Trees" as appearing in *The Eye Like a Strange Balloon* copyright © 2004 by Mary Jo Bang. Used by permission of Grove/Atlantic, Inc.

Published by Graywolf Press
2402 University Avenue, Suite 203
Saint Paul, Minnesota 55114
All rights reserved.

www.graywolfpress.org

Published in the United States of America

ISBN 978-1-55597-483-1

2 4 6 8 9 7 5 3 1
First Graywolf Printing, 2007

Library of Congress Control Number: 2007924768

Cover design: Christa Schoenbrodt, Studio Haus
Creative direction: David Schuman
Cover art: Michael Donner Van Hook, *Firing the Neurons*
            Photographed by David Ulmer

CONTENTS

For

Michael Donner Van Hook

January 17, 1967 – June 21, 2004

ELEGY

A SONATA FOR FOUR HANDS

Causes and consequences line up,
Ready for the next dawn
With its blight

Of glass bulbs.
In the welled nothingness of definitely,
There is another

Sad sobbing day. Someone has seen you
And says you were fine
Just hours before you weren't.

I say Come Back and you do
Not do what I want.
The train unrolls its track and sends its sound forward.

The siren unrolls its sound and sends itself
Forward. The first day of the last goes forward
As the last summer you'll see.

The dirge is all wrong for the season. Death remains
Wedded to mystery. How
Does the heart stop? On what

Moment's turning?
Which tick? And why? Only where
Is settled. Behind an address. Some block

Building. Some barricade brick
That hides bracketed hours
Until the doom door opens

And my I sees.
Police seal peeled back. Everything
As you left it. On and over and under.

Why are you not where you belong?
A black hat on a hook says nothing.
Ashes mirror ashes

In a mirroring window. And now how
Do we resolve this predicament?
The body becomes the art

Of identity. A face
In a photograph. The bas relief
Around the morgue door.

You, singularly you. And gone
Invisible.

A SONATA FOR FOUR HANDS, II

The lights in the shades were lit,
Each bulb became
An empty symbol waiting
Like the fixed idea
Above a comic book Mickey. Outside,
Clouds connived to create obscure messages:
Here's a giraffe.

A male lion has a mane.
Imagination's ridiculous art.
She was clearly a member
Of the fiasco survivor's club
The living often belong to.
There a simple name meant, simply,
A name. No allegory. No

Discursive meaning.
Just experience. No interpretation
Possible, nor necessary.
Condense to seven stanzas
A particulate world. Draw a picture
Of flesh engineered
As parts of a whole. The pills

On the floor had rolled under the sofa.
The wheel begins its *if only* turning.
It had never stopped.
This is life's bargain that motion
Is hope. Morning fog,
Come back again. You will dream
Of this. Undoubtedly.

Quiet. Of course.
The audience eyes were all waiting to lock
Onto the future.

The sayings got said in a voice
That was almost a quiver.
There were references to the serpentine

After. The greens were all perfectly pretty
Green. As in spring.
The snake of time was spending itself

Like an arrow in motion, aimed at a bale of hay,
Each bale a bad day. Then wham, and over.
The absence sandblasted.

They all stood next to a ledge
From which everyone could see
The river of a personal history

Undermining the roots of To Be.
Do you see? An immanent fall
After which a loved one could no longer be

Picked up and propped up and kept up
Against something that kept breaking free.
In the vacancy the world went on revolving.

And somebody was no longer thinking,
It's lovely. It's rich.
In the mind's photographic eye

He still looked like he was, but he wasn't.
And then, Look at us
Here in the after-funeral, she said. We're staring

At the open-mouthed stars,
The cars crawling on Twentieth, reduced
To pairs of brights and no more.

We're remembering to set an alarm
On tomorrow. We're forgetting the bad
Days of crumbling rocks in our stockings at x-mas.

Someone shook her
Awake and she rose and went on.

Goodbye to forever now.
Hello to the empty present and.
Goodbye to the orchids woven
With something that looks like a seed weed.

Hello to the day
We looked out through
The juniper smudge
Burned to remember the moment.

The doctoring moment is over.
A sheaf of paper drops like lead
From the tree of the table it came from.
The eyes play tricks.

The quilt edge clasped in the hand
Goes on and on and on.
Rumination is this. You
A child, then a man, now a feather

Passing through a furious fire
Called time. The cone of some plant
From a place I don't know
In the high flames.

Rumination is and won't stop
With the stoppered bottle, the pills
On the floor, the broken plate
On the floor, the sleeping face

In the bassinette of your birth month,
The dog bite, the difficulty,
The stairwell of a three-flat
Of your sixth year, the flood

Of farthering off this all takes you
As thought and object become
What you are. My stoppered mind.
A voice, carried by machine,

Across a lifeless body. Across
A lacerating lapse in time.

WAITING

Was distinctly unglamorous.
A wince-making barrenness.
An eighteen-rib mule

Hungry unfed at the empty.
It wasn't an imaginary landscape.
But the morgue man bent

Over the young man asleep on a Lethean slab.
It was the season of quiet:
The quiet of death. The uneasy quiet

After the gasp in the middle
Of the terrible, terrible movie
That someone had made and kept showing

On the screen at the back of her mind.
She would watch it now,
Its implacable Technicolor patterns,

Gray shirt, green pants,
The forced metal deco trim of a door.
The open door leading always to darkness.

UTOPIAN LONGING BECOMES MORE ABSURD

After the beloved is dead.
After the personal history ends
With a glassy-eyed over, it's been,
Says a polar presence. Cold

Juxtaposes with the waning warmth
Of the human. Cold, and its polar
Opposite. There was once
An earlier epoch

Of four-wheeled skates, a Philadelphia
Sidewalk, when imagination corresponded
To a future. Here is the tormented
Arithmetic of one minus one. The zero

In one now hides the other. This is
What it looks like. A domino sequence
Of nothing becoming a spectacle
Watched for a while

(The gate latch sticks and then clicks)
While eating a cone of cotton candy.

THE CRUEL WHEEL TURNS TWICE

And tightens until language can't bear this
Hollowing, crash cart, Please. In the silence,
A bus slithers by

A din. The aluminum morning takes on more tension
And becomes a metal rod
Straight from a tunnel, dropped in a gate groove.

Disappointment. And again The End gate
Opens and it's, Please
Come back. Please Be. Then nothing. Only end-

Less night taking off from the smooth tarmac slate.
The potpie clock, its stock of twelve numbers,
A stew for the weak and the weary.

The small war of the heart made bigger
by far in the world.
And daylight a gift.

Small cog after cog slips into the hour
And razor thin minute slot without stop.
And daylight a gift tied with some tinsel.

BENEATH THE DIN

Of voices bouncing off
Hard walls and window
Wall and tile surface on which feet, two

Per person, rest and chair legs, four
Per chair, rest, there is breath.
Talk is to be

Human again. Silence is an escape
Page as white as a tablet
Of Phenobarbital. There is no waking

Up from death. That's the pity.
The dead leave what could be
Next unfinished.

You left nothing
Left to say and yet there is this
Incomplete labyrinth

Of finished thought, this
Wash of days over energy's uneven rock. This
Vault door's hollow closing

Crash behind which I say, Stop,
To the accidental.
Uncle, to the twisty wrist.

Eyes, close, to the insomnia hour. Then
Tomorrow merges with the present
And becomes the possibility

Of the vacuumed after
Where a snake makes its way back
Across a game table sea of emerald green leaves.

The guest clouds circle and soak up the night
And all the ghosts go blank.

WHAT IS SO FRIGHTENING

She said as the cab passed the building
She'd passed in her childhood, is pathos.
Its mean little whip of pity. The force filled
With persistence demanding dominance.
The plate changing. The green moved over
And made room for emptiness.

The storm scream came and went.
Comes and goes. The warm day was caught
In a watch. And now the yellow car
Was passing near another corner she knew.
Time called her attention. There was
Someone like this before, she thought.

Upstanding, blank-faced, red-dressed.
Someone sitting in a box, defining herself
As one with roots. One burnished
By expandable light. One busied with examining
A nasty bruise. One who was becoming
Part of a past. One for whom

Ever-ending had suddenly become ever
The end. And now nightly the void, empty and devoid
Of starry ornamentation. Paxil's myoclonal kick
Shifting the bedclothes slightly toward
The ghost at the side of the bed who speaks from within
The white sheet trademark of tragedy.

WHERE

In this cicada city, we are dead,
We are quiet, we are home.
Here, you belong

To me. I, to you. The trees lurch
Toward later summer, reach
Toward the window

Where glass makes a mirror
Of the sitting. Lightning forks.
All directions lead to my empty head

Bent over a box of cicatrix ash.
My mothering lips are stitched
Shut by sorrow.

What was once a mind
Is pried open.
Look, doctor, at the tangle

Of synapse
Where the pearl should be.
And then, distraction —

The pink Mobius strip dips down
And begins its torturous twist.
The current catches

The tree and drags me forward
Toward the missing beginning.

ODE TO HISTORY

Had she not lain on that bed with a boy
All those years ago, where would they be, she wondered.
She and the child that wouldn't have been but was now
No more. She would know nothing
Of mothering. She would know nothing
Of death. She would know nothing
Of love. The three things she'd been given
To remember. Wake me up, please, she said,
When this life is over. Look at her — It's as if
The windows of night have been sewn to her eyes.

A PLACE

He was one of the bottomward stars
That settled on the seabed.
Twice reflected. The real and the partial.
Like water and a water-lined slide.

He'd already slid
Into a depression. Into the state of wishing
To be all he had been which was now but a blur.
Haze on the way to becoming a cloud.

Or better, a place where we feel the body's heat
As the temperature of the forehead
We place our hand against.
The back of the hand as it meets

Becomes the flesh we had ceased to feel. I'm sorry.
For the things I regret. The two rounds
In the ring. Before and after. The castle
And the riverward rat. We've gone so far

Afield now. You are fire and air
And I am tin. We will never meet again.
Here, drink this little bit
Of Lethe water.

SEPTEMBER IS

September is work to the center
Of arguments and controversies.
Prejudgments and incomprehensions.
What will I love if not that
That was enigma?
The years of infancy, Memory says,
And there we are, with the demon
Of the art of living
Traced on the glass of some window.

In the beauty of the night of May,
Clear of moon, to the lume of a candle
There was a design like the profile
Of a landscape almost abandoned. Gone
But not gone yet. It's fascinating,
These mysterious uncovered feelings.
Enigma of an afternoon of autumn, the picture
Of which is a composition
Of the eye of my mind. Every hour

That I watch this picture
I see again still that moment.
Nevertheless the moment is an enigma
For me, in how much is inexplicable.
The physical things hide in the architecture
Of the event. The enigma of a mock-up,
Of a shadow, the spectral and eternal aspect
Of the moment. Praises to you for being
One great box of surprise,

Your head the scene of a wonderful theater
Of the most tender gray of the fog
That joins the sky to the earth.
A tangling of truth and memory,
Mythology and iconography,
I watch with the eye
Of the mind the city that accommodates
That one beautiful day that is now infinite.
It deepens. It begins. The cyclical method.

Memory is deeply not alive; it's a mock-up
And this renders it hateful. Yet, it is not a fiction,
Is a truth, indeed a sad and monstrous truth.
I was assigned to you, together we were
A beautiful and melancholic picture.
This last picture is the realization
Of the overwhelming moment
In which the acute eye perceives you as a now
That is over. A now that is now fixed
In the swept past.

ENCLOSURE

Who knew that a police seal was blue,
That a morgue door could have metal deco trim
Around its rectangular invitation
To come in have a seat and complete this

Form. That was June. Now is the cusp
Of October where you teeter
On the brink of a date marking more
Sorrow in store. More days

With an off-white ice rink sky
Of winter waiting.
The clock with its digital blinking
Is also a pathetic asking for more.

Words keep slipping away, so many
Ice blocks in a scene of whiteness,
A mood of Sweden, bleeding
Trees breaking down

Because they are ice-covered.
Little idiosyncratic expressions can form
A sense of who one is. Who one was.
One can, hypothetically, be brought back

In the form of an actor

Who gives an after the fact replication
Of text conveyed in a character's voice.
I can no more understand the world as a stage
Of myself, mired as I am,

In this missing. The missing is married
To drizzle. Of course, tears
Are only one aspect
Of the scenery of sorrow. The language

Of ancestors, mourning the departure
Of any or many. This October, every day ends
With five o'clock dimness
Sealing the landscape into a tin.

The outside comes in
The window, or I go out the door.
Nothing matters
To the ash in the box.

It asks for more nothing and instead
Gets a heel-click reminder
That one of us is still here.
At least until the next amazing cessation.

Sight and sound. Sight and sound.
And the mind's drugged blunt.

DEFINITELY

What is desire
But the hardwire argument given
To the mind's unstoppable mouth.

Inside the braincase, it's I
Want that fills every blank. And then the hand
Reaches for the pleasure

The plastic snake offers. Someone says, Yes,
It will all be fine in some future soon.
Definitely. I've conjured a body

In the chair before me. Be yourself, I tell it.
Here memory makes you
Unchangeable: that shirt, those summer pants.

That beautiful face.
That tragic beautiful mind.
That mind's ravenous mouth

That told you, This isn't poison
At all but just what the machine needs. And then,
The mouth closes on its hunger.

The heart stops.

LANDSCAPE WITH THE FALL OF ICARUS

How could I have failed you like this?
The narrator asks

The object. The object is a box
Of ashes. How could I not have saved you,

A boy made of bone and blood. A boy
Made of a mind. Of years. A hand

And paint on canvas. A marble carving.
How can I not reach where you are

And pull you back. How can I be
And you not. You're forever on the platform

Seeing the pattern of the train door closing.
Then the silver streak of me leaving.

What train was it? The number 6.
What day was it? Wednesday.

We had both admired the miniature mosaics
Stuck on the wall of the Met.

That car should be forever sealed in amber.
That dolorous day should be forever

Embedded in amber.
In garnet. In amber. In opal. In order

To keep going on. And how can it be
That this means nothing to anyone but me now.

THREE TREES

The aqua green goes with the pink
in a way no one knows what will happen.
Every step is a dangerous taking.
Amazing the time span of a trunk
(a door opens in it and suddenly,
someone is asking how this came to be).
The green curtain is a pressed chime
which when rung rings in a dogwood
white as if a storm were approaching
its green extreme.

Brick crumbles into living pond particle
while a bent hook holds back
the last dissolve.
An uneasy leap over a sharky sea.
Gravity plays its little emotive role.
It's Elm Street all over
again, ragged walkways lead to Toon Town.
Hello kids. Hello Jimmy Neutron.
The blanket rises, and under it,
a fetishistic pompadour

green, greener and paler than bluebird.
But hush, the nuclear power plant
is about to blow unless
Jimmy can locate the elusive button.
A siren and standing-by fire truck.
It looks like a lost cause until presto,
a messenger. A racketing aside.
The day is dragged here and there but still
can't be saved. BAM. Immediately
the next second clicks into the skyscape

apocalypse. In the dust, a celluloid woman
mows a multilayered lawn.
The arch overhead reads, O Art
Still Has Truth Take Refuge. Where? There.
There, there, says someone.

ONCE

Once there was my life and it was a thing
Filled with difficulty but it was mine.
Now *Now* is a terrible ongoing and some-
Times I consider the alternative. Yes,
The x on the ash box says,
I know what you mean. Somewhere
A sound crackles under the mean
Sky of mid-to-late October. Broke bough of one
Limb. Lambikin, let's go back
To the beginning. You keep reminding me
That I said I would never leave you to the monster
Whom greed has now brought out from under
His ogre-log. We all fail each other sometime.
See how vague language can pretend to be.
See how exact intention is.

NOVEMBER ELEGY

November is more of the usual
November. Sheets of rain
Cut into tidy rectangular grays.
Ghostly sections of cemetery pall.

The cymbal of morning is secretary
To each idiomatic new day.
I wake up and go walking.
From the front of my mind I see a garden

With a half-living yellow lily,
A pinkish-rose rose,
A deadheaded daisy.
Personal history is fiction but in spite of that

There are those simple elements
Of a singular experiment.
To say the minute is manufactured
Inside a clock, what does that mean?

That time is nothing more
Than a lame recomposed, after the fact,
Potential? Silence takes no as an answer.

SHE REMEMBERS HIS HAT

The quality of time is "poor."
An abstraction that dissolves
Of its own accord.
There is no language

Unique to time. Devoted. Addicted.
The claustrophobic "because." Just sit
In darkness and watch the world
Illuminated on a screen. It's all

I ask of you. You are now
Only an aspect
Of my brain. My eyes
See you. The balance of what you are

And what you do—the syntax
Of inaction versus the syntax
Of deliberate action
Is distorted into a state of loose coherence

In the theater of the skull where
Joined stills speak to the plastic memory.
Your head bent over a book.
Your exit.

Iconic scenes undercut the ordinary.
The hat on its hook. The clock intercut.

THE WATCH

Argus's eyes in the tail of the peacock are watching
Over us. We're at the Zoo of Human Proportions.
We're caged. We're handled. We're always
Wanting some little treat
Proffered by one in a clean coat. A carrot. A harlot

Looking over us. The owl is cheeky, also wise.
It is over. We've mapped our lives. This is the attempt.
The song uncertain because behind the curtain,
The musical background is the blasphemous
Batty woman at the subway stop

Serving us up her scrap of discourse.
A game. A tournament. Turn to me
One last time. A hug. A goodbye. An I love you.
All bathed in the neon spiteful irony
Of the Bowery's day for night. When the scene is done

Whatever we have is almost over. The end.
The lights close their stupid white eyes
On the cruel inaccuracy of an end that was meant
To happen much later but didn't. It happened soon
After when the held danger broke like light

On water churning over someone going under.

JANUARY ELEGY

There is this still, night-coming, beautiful horizon,
Birds gunning up and the dead grass
That means winter is still

Here and held in its dull intent.
Within minutes, the horizon is no longer
A flat gradation of gray

With a hint of silver mirror decay.
Instead, it's absence black.
And the moment is made up of car brights

And music sending a sound wave from inside
The mind. Nothing is stopping.
A year in tatters is interrupted by the thought

That the future is manacled
To the indefatigable now of February.
Still as the knife-girl strapped to the circle spinning,

Her hair splayed to one side.
Her eyes empty behind the blindfold.
The sense of silk. Her heart stopped.

NO EXIT

The story is written,
Here is the kingdom—castle and castle
Turret seen from a train. The interruption

To the ongoing sight line.
She had come from being the slip
Of a girl without a clue to someone

Who knew. She came from the room.
On the table, the empty vessel of the word "missing"
In figurative and literal language.

I miss. You are missing to me. Minor variation
In foreign syntax systems.
Someone once told her that spring meant green

Was on the stem of every flower.
This was the springless January of his beginning
To be gone forever.

Who was to say what cohesion held
Together? Cells strung along some string theory.
They say I. She said,

Will the cigarette girl who told me what Sartre said
Please tell me again?
Someone has spun me around, I don't know where

I'm going. What is today? Where am I?
What cruel nature wires a brain like this?
To give it pleasure

And then let pleasure make itself a pain?
To say you loved a person.
To say that person no longer exists.

A tragic flawed fate going on and on and on.

DON'T

Try to speak
For more than yourself, he'd told her. Fine.
A bit of Goodnight. A bit of Hello. A little bit of Later.

But wasn't there a lesson to be learned
From listening. In watching
The night creep up on the noon. The soon vanishing

In the end where death dissolved the one.
That's where things went wrong.
Is went into language. A daughter was. A son said.

Things still did happen. Continuation. Morning
Replaced night's green beginning.
Dreamland kept getting larger. It expanded

To embrace both time and timelessness.
One minute left on the steps and told to be still,
Another minute sent to a misaligned elsewhere.

So, life. So, self-replication
Of the synaptic blip. A leap and a miss.
The lip makes its tremble.

Again and again. It sounded like rumination
To her. The less the terrible
Missing was refashioned into emptiness,

The better. A scenario: A month of small candy
Red hearts could stand for the sear through the mind
Of transient affection.

The better the missing was refashioned into pure emptiness,
The less the terrible. She would traverse an eon and ever
The dead one would stay as he was.

That was the knife.
In a somewhere park where one walks and walks to get nowhere,
Except where one has walked, a banner flapped behind her,

Flipping like a fabric moment. It was the start
Of the baton and the dirge drum.
This was the end. The circle of an O that looked like a life

Had hasped shut. Everything became logical when
It was strung up like a string of lights. Bright
Beginning, bright middle, bright end. And out.

You want the whole story? I'll begin
At the beginning. It was January. Troy was under
Siege. It was about to come down.

It was not about sound
At all, but the fall of the heart
From its sky-height position.

Remember the cat Lewis Carroll sent
To look in on Alice at least once a week
As she found what she found

Difficult to decipher. A gesture
Of sympathy, yes, yet nowhere could she find comfort.
What might have seemed like a symphony was not

That at all but some interior quartz-pitched bewailing.
"What if, she thought, it all hadn't happened
The way it did?" She placed that notion on the Mobius strip

And watched it go nowhere before it came back again.
A melancholic introspection retrospective
Was taking place in a white-walled room called Summer Was.

THE GAME

Begins with hints of menace, birth violence first, then
Struggle ensues until: At last,
The hero or heroine pulls a sword and then
There is the blood that signs the end

Of life as we knew it—afraid and more
Afraid. Darling sleep and Doris Day
Cheerfulness now follows
Us to the other end

Which is happy and handholding.
But eventually we wake to No (know)
It's only sleep so must be done again.
The story circles

Its tail, just missing its mouth, over and over,
A moving production of *At last, At last, At last*—
Each "At last" followed by waking
To a day and dodging the enemy which looks like a face

In a mirror—two ears, two eyes, and an act.
Until we get to feeling
Who cares anymore
About virtuosity and we lay down the sword

And say to the ghost we are giving it up,
We are stopping. And we do
And finally we are happy after—and finally
Fatally so. Please close the game board.

Please hide the little pieces.

FEBRUARY ELEGY

This bald year, frozen now in February.
This cold day winging over the ugly
Imperfect horizon line,
So often a teeth line of ten buildings.
A red flag flapping
In the wind. An orange curtain is noon.
It all hurts her eyes. This curtain is so bright.
Here is what is noticeably true: sight.
The face that looks back from the side
Of the butter knife.
A torn-bread awkwardness.
The mind makes its daily pilgrimage
Through riff-raff moments. Then,
Back into the caprice case to dream
In a circle, a pony goes round.
The circle's association: There's a center
To almost everything but never
Any certainty. Nothing is
More malleable than a moment. We were
Only yesterday breathing in a sea.
Some summer sun
Asked us over and over we went. The sand was hot.
We were only yesterday tender hearted
Waiting. To be something.
A spring. And then someone says, Sit down,
We have a heart for you to forget. A mind to suffer
With. So, experience. So, the circus tent.
You, over there, you be the girl
In red sequins on the front of a card selling love.
You, over there, you, in black satin,
You be the Maiden's Mister Death.

HELL

These earthly flourishes have taken root
As a silver streak machine-age train bearing down.
I hear nothing in the see-nothing night but sense motion.

The exquisite ache for the one
Half-hidden in the tree, leaves at his feet.
Fallen leaves and lost senses.

Eyes and ears
And a brain. The delicate elegant brain that dreams
Of a train that stops for nothing.

I had a lifetime. After which a murder of craven angels
Appeared dressed as crows.
Small heads and wingspans

Formed a straightedge measuring
Here and distinguishing it
In the small ways it can be

From the territory over there where
Men covered the world and dark came
Down, blanketing and blanking out the sun

And the sad and sorry. Monday will never come again.
Sing a Song of Sixpence.
These birds eat and eat. Everything.

TRAGEDY

It begins to sink in. Dead
Is dead, not just not
Here. The knife never dulls,
Does it, Dearie,
On the blade side.

Now the daily face-rain is over
The edge of a moment.
The ash box and I bide our time.
This is typical. This is classical.
This is what tragedy was

Always trying to teach us.
Those toga-wrapped torsos,
That chattering
Chorus, those women
With Psyche-knots in the center

Of a circular stage,
Under an Athenian sun,
Foreign enough now to confound
The eye that knows nothing
Of them but what comes crawling

Larva-like out of a book.
In yesterday's dream
We and others all
Wrapped ourselves in sheets
And went flying. Something

Like Peter Pan. Something
Like a child who will always be
A child. Who would never grow up
And who now never will become
Because his eyes have been

Ceased shut and will not open ever.

TO ASH

The dustpan of dirt bits is near over.
Bring me a broom. A broom
Is bright. We can't stop remembering
Pleasure, can we? The escape

Through the plate glass to the green grass
Of the other side. No more.
Which is what done means.
Has always meant.

The pain is—and now make your own list. It's this
And it's that. Tsunami and suicide. Please
Takes its mate
And together they make Please and Thank you.

And someone takes that text and attaches it
To blue board, acid free and lasting.
And there you have it, a life
That makes you forget for the moment

This is your one and only
Mechanically insistent pulse. Otherwise,
Every circle is turned to looking up
And every crossing over is

An endless plain of remembering
That the overcast sky is merely the secondary drama
On the screen at the back of the mind, and far
From the real eye's vigilant watch

For a reliable means of distraction.
If only an actor could stand in for the self
Nothing bad would happen.

THERE IS NO PRETENDING

There is no pretending to know
What crawls out of the mind lying quiet
By itself in the snow of the grave grass.
The living know this alone:
The onomatopoetic *fout-ta-ta-rou* of the mitral valve
Inferred but not felt by a mind that has left
Itself to others. Decisionless and dull, I am one
With the glass-bound aluminum clouds
In a glitter-knitted metallica sky. I live on
The bite of air that follows a door's night close
And the dusky base of the thumbnail that darkens
As it presses down on earth fading away beneath
It. Pax, peace. Axe, beat
Of the heart and its dumb numbered afterecho.

THE OPENING

1.

Open the door and look in.
Everything is in place.
The flicking heart
The owlet eyes are locked on.
A serpentine hair hangs over an ear.
A hand comes up to touch it.
A rhythmic hum runs ahead of the wave.
Someone turns her head
And hopes, no, lopes across the lawn.

2.

Open the door and look in.
The black magic cat is clawing the sofa.
The midnight lamp is loosing some light.
Someone is getting undressed.
Her pajamas are pressed
And she's getting into a bed of flowers.
Ophelia is lying in the bog in the park,
A moment's orphan in the afterdark.
Sing me a song, Pet, I beg of you.

3.

Open the door and look in.
The Vivian Girls are reading the books
Their countenances were cut from.
It's like a mirror. The parent and the penguin
Child. Two men with two suitcases.
The hand mirror making its lake
Last as long as it can.

The self looking the depth
Of Wallace Stevens' wife on the dime.

4.

Open the door and look in.
A murder, some mayhem, the night
News. A cloak on a hook in the closet.
There's no rug on the floor and the wood
Feels warm. There may have been an arson.
Mistakenly Released Suspect Still Missing
In Dogville or Dogtown or the Down-and-out
Sorry state of things now. Listen,
Brenda Lee is singing, I'm sorry.

5.

Open the door and look in. Look
Down the page to the footnote. To the fine print.
To the FedEx box on the bedside and
The floral print jammies that are jarring
Against the previous-era paper on the wall.
Some ice-cream topper Jimmies
To top off the night. Red Yellow Blue White.
The deer-leg lamp, says Jessica, really does work
And with that, she twirls the shade like a top.

6.

Open the door and look in.
A pin under the bed.
A dust layer on the desk top.
The minutia and microbe, the fear of failing

To ward off the inevitable, It will be done.
Whatever the It is. The static of darkness,
The dissolve of the moment.
The mouse crawls out of its house,
Remembers where it last ate a grub.

7.

Open the door, Mother, and look in.
The babies in their boxes are sleeping like beetles
In ladybug red, each with a Santa hat.
They're all at the border of risk,
All about to vanish into the past
Of the unvarnished after.
A longer word for gone. Girl.
Boy. Girl. Boy. Girl. Boy.
If we turn out the lights, they will keep.

8.

Open the door and look in.
In her pajamas, she looks thin.
Pale skin, short nails, hail on the rooftop
And window glass. January is ant dark
Every morning and early in the late afternoon.
With a gloom aspect like a seascape
That was smoke damaged above a fire grate.
The wrapped-mummy mood mutes
The emo that spins like a Catherine Wheel.

9.

Open the door and look back.
Over your shoulder. A peach-cheek
Love bird on a cage roost
Is swinging back and forth.
He's nature, but he also seems nervous.
The traffic din music comes floating in.
He's nature, but he also seems nervous.
Sing us a song, Pet, and he does. He sings of arson
In Alexandria, of Helen of Tragic of Troy.

HEARTBREAKING

The mechanical bird on the back
Of the taxidermy wolf.
Nature is all act,

All dustbin diorama glass case at the end
Of a corridor, the case standing on a leg,
The bear claw balanced

On a man-made marble ball. The case against
The entry hall wall. Is it possible
To leave this world?

Only if you leave out science.
Seawater drips off the lip of a wave
And refills the sea. Tomorrow, the lacerated

Lifeline. Wish-fish, wish-fish, speak to me.
Give me my last wish.
The wind as a bullet

Is lodged in my brain.
A tangle in the branches. Death is the lot
With an abyss at the edge. A raven

Hovers above. The imagination caught
In the door latch.
How much does matter matter? Very.

"IN ORDER" MEANS NEAT AND NOT NEXT

Night was next. At some point
On the train the outside dissolved
And she was sitting next to herself in a seat.
In a two-tone gray and blue vinyl seat
With hints of a previous sitter. The dim other
She'd tried so hard to revive but failed
Was staring back at her

Through grit and dirt glass.
These are my footprints, she thought,
Looking at her feet, Mary Jo's in Mary Janes.
Made of parts, they nullified the notion of total
Wholeness. The absurd road was obliterated
And all of the moment was inside.
The body buried in time.

Time, a fickle list of numbers.
Sleep was the utopian fantasy
She wished she could fall into.
Eye to the window, to fate.
Feeling but not seeing. Out there was absence
And presence. Out there was a row
Of everything she remembered.

A sea, a shipside and then, a later scene, at the center of empti-ness: her hair floats up but never meets the horizon line. She's sinking, behind the drape of the dead day and later on, after that, wearing a nightdress. Once, when I was four, in a fever, I saw someone not there. I see you as a grief heat hallucination telling me I could have saved you if I'd been better. Then, a hand-ful of tablets. The curtain comes down on the handcuffed one. The end, the end. Yet again. Overshadowed by history, destruc-tion is all. Design a lake. Place it at the edge of a city. Think of it as a door. Then let yourself in. A film made of frames shows the variations of hours that slide through time like a hand-wound camera slides film through a slot, until it stops on the sprockets and holds. Then the moment is a packaged magazine pose. Ancient and every and over. Both more and the same as any particular image invented: fantasy and scientific fact, death and its problems, cases of trance mistaken for death.

INTRACTABLE, AND IRREVERSIBLE

The overcast cast of the sky is the secondary drama.
On the screen at the back of the mind.
Far from the vigilant eye,

A dictionary definition of death is written
Over the grid of a calendar sequence.
Death is the date when the output is over.

An irreversible heartbeat hiatus
That goes by the name of no more.
At home in his ash box, he was going nowhere

Else. He was living with her now
In a land of low clouds
Where weather was the only change she could hope for.

The clouds see nothing.
The clouds are nothing but ice changes and water.
Water changes and morning's cold sets in motion

The proximate—the visible—day.
There will be no more of time and time's corruption
For the ash in the box. The love of her life.

She notices how quiet he is in there.
Out here, she says, I talk
But always to a mirror

Where a face looks out like a clock that says night
Is coming and then it comes like a coat of silted black.
Thank you, she says, as she slips into bed.

One more alarm silenced. One more
Closet door closed. One more
Shoe sole set to the floor

Of checkered linoleum. The castle is quiet, the castle is snug.
A dream bell begins to toll, to tell
Of the intolerable end that keeps going on.

TALK TO ME

Talk to me, he said.
The narrative begins and we fill in the blanks.
The kind of grammar. The color and tone
Of the tense. There's always an exception
But there's always a rule.
The rudderless language

Of everyday life.
Talk to me and tell me, what
In the world. This from the man
Who would turn to a stone.
Like Sisyphus, she nudges her child
Until he is again back above

The disaster chasm horizon line.
The rain has been held off a notch.
The stage sun is devised
From the mote load of a flood lamp lumen.
A dollie drags the lamp back
Until the yellow dot becomes a lot

More. Which side of the lake, he asks,
Is the near side of Lethe?

WORDS

Parole. Mote in one's own eye. The deceit
That a lifetime is. I wasn't there
When something happened. Something

Happened. A chair was pushed out from a table.
Don't listen if you don't want to know
What happened, the Sergeant said. I don't want to know

The future as it's seen on that inked slip of paper
That says one has only now and no more.
It was fourth grade or fifth.

Or it was eighth grade or the grade up the side
Of the river or the ditch at the side of the road.
It was very steep. It's always been difficult.

Breath like a hollow rasp but almost silent.
A management that keeps one sane. A hand gliding
An iron over a piece of fabric.

Like skates, like a sewing stitch
Done to keep one's attention from wavering.
The self talking to a mirror.

All the doctors know that. The ones who see you lying
On a sofa. They know that there is a sound
In one's head. They know there is that deep

Relief from the waking state called sleep. How little else
They know unless you tell them. I tell them
I wish I could lie under the summer.

UNTITLED

The story is written, the slip of a girl is loosed
And her life folds over. Against the cold, the waiting
For the what will happen. The next. Wonderful
Awful. The blonde in a chemical bath.
The story keeps on being written
As a woman who waits for never to happen
As an empty wall waits for light to form a bridge
And under it, a mass of open eyes,
Waiting for the awful eventual. Now?
And yes is what is said. Then here it is, the box
We live in where the crazy face of the day looks back
At the closed eye of the night looking in.
A boy of four comes in as an example
Of where the door of life is left open for a moment.
Time tumbles hour after hour until it's morning again.
Some glass is for looking through, some is for seeing back.
Every outline is a cage one way or another.

WHAT IF

Fate always had this waiting
In the middle of the road we were riding toward.

A myth character with her face
Nasty with persimmon and fig.

You with a handful of Phenobarbital tablets.
You with a need

To escape the too much. What if
Fate means no fault

Designed as an arrow in the heart of forever.
Then it might be easier.

We could eat the asphalt sandwich
And go on toward some happy hamlet hearth and home.

Some dreamless sleeps. I don't believe in fate.
What if fate were a voice saying,

This is how they'll live now.
In a bank-vault.

He'll be obedient and she'll be intractable.
And dead. It's all they ever wanted.

A BOY AT PLAY IS AN ACTOR IN A TRAGEDY

This was the drama
Of impossibility. The congress
Of humorless solutions.
He would be no sepia set
Of nostalgic names making up an inimitable signature.
No metaphysical stone in the hand
Of the haunted and mad.
He was defined by now
And now was negation.

She was full of restlessness.
Of erratic thought.
She kept waking thinking
No less today than a year ago.
No less then than at the beginning.
In the photograph, the soft mask of his fixed
Expression hinted at a connoisseurship
Of difficulty. Like myth.
Like the ramshackle

Brushstrokes of the painting
On the wall. Distance and all
Was simply an idea. Both a hollow
Promised location.
(Please be.)
And an equivocation. Here we are,
She said to the box next to her desk,
And here we will be, on-and-on-
Living in the realm of simultaneity.

GOODBYE IS ANOTHER WORD FOR NOT

Imagine the movie
With its seen scene. It's 5:15
And what's left of life.
That realization is a real formula

For reluctance.
The sun is still a lemon
Rim around a rectangle
Window shade. Everybody's

Subject is sitting in his or her seat.
A bonfire of burnt-orange burns
At the bottom of the screen.
It's fall so

It's the bonfire of exquisite trees
With russet leaves.
Minnie's whitegloved hand reaches
Out to touch

A leaf leafleting down.
And in that, evidence of
The bitter coil's poor mistress
Of unceasing seasons. Someone says,

What day is it? No one answers.
The cold beauty in the middle
Section of the seats,
Her smile pinned up

Like a pretty girl smiles
Out as the character, perfection acting
For all of us, says,
At the end of the day,

The sun always goes away.
She is lying on the edge of nothing.
When we exit, outside, an orange light
On the top of a cab is something. ,

Nothing less than incandescence.
That bright and that almost
Over. And then, we see the evil
Denouement: as the movie apparatus

Matches the lumenaire taxi light,
Making them both disappear.
How sad is absence. How very gone
The nothing after.

NOW

Now, she said, do you know
How I feel? No, he said,

I know nothing.
I'm only, as you've described me,

Ash in a box. No, she said,
That's not what I meant

When I said that. You are everything
And that. It's ironic

Language that has described you that way.
You are reduced

To the after-sorrow
That will last my lifetime. The hair-tearing

Grief of the mother
Whose child has been swept away

By the needle broom
Of all her mindless errors.

What she'd meant to say was that
The body as ash is inadequate.

SHE SAID

It felt like a frequency
Went through her, her head
Came up and her mind went
Clear. That was earlier. Later,
It was as if life were being lived
In the afterglow of a starburst
With the remnants
Of a collapsed star creating
A fast-spinning solar corpse
That left as an aftermath
Of the blast, a smoldering
Oblong ring that would glow
For light years, the debris
Launching itself into the surrounding
Air and swallowing everything
In its wake. Wake up, she told herself.
He wouldn't want you to dream
The rest of your life into the fictional
Transactions that happen
Only in dreams.
But there she was, sadder yet
On gray days, slightly less when the sun shone
Bright. December and November were gone.
January brought his birthday
Which was missed and would be forever.
Then that stupid red day
Where roses were themselves,
Over and over again, and wrapped
In a cone of slick paper.
March and April were waiting
To be something like a beginning

That repeats every year some Persephone
Story of a cell-phone phone-home
To say the future will be
Okay and mother please pray for me
Now as I travel across another green sea.

THE ROLE OF ELEGY

The role of elegy is
To put a death mask on tragedy,
A drape on the mirror.
To bow to the cultural

Debate over the aesthetization of sorrow,
Of loss, of the unbearable
Afterimage of the once material.
To look for an imagined

Consolidation of grief
So we can all be finished
Once and for all and genuinely shut up
The cabinet of genuine particulars.

Instead there's the endless refrain
One hears replayed repeatedly
Through the just ajar door:
Some terrible mistake has been made.

What is elegy but the attempt
To rebreathe life
Into what the gone one once was
Before he grew to enormity.

Come on stage and be yourself,
The elegist says to the dead. Show them
Now—after the fact —
What you were meant to be:

The performer of a live song.
A shoe. Now bow.
What is left but this:
The compulsion to tell.

The transient distraction of ink on cloth
One scrubbed and scrubbed
But couldn't make less.
Not then, not soon.

Each day, a new caption on the cartoon
Ending that simply cannot be.
One hears repeatedly, the role of elegy is.

WE ARE ONLY HUMAN

Nighttime amnesia.
The dream becoming
Cartoonish and mint-sequined.

A caboose climbing an emerald hill.
Daily we tend the garden.
Daily we wave

Our lashes like little flags
In a cordial wind. I? Who isn't
Ever I in a circular now.

The toothbrush is ready.
The mouth comes to meet it.
Life begins and goes on.

The fall is always waiting.
We're the always drifting above.

WHERE ONCE

On the street, looking up, there you were.
A single helium balloon, imagine
A flat-face mouse in Mylar.

You floated the way you always liked to float.
Now you have been renamed and imperfectly faced.
You've become the extreme form of nothingness

Sequestered, as at the end of a siege
In a quarantined city hospitals are often reduced
To ideas and empty rooms.

You're still there for those who know where to look
And what to watch for, as in dreams—where
In spite of death color comes back,

Youth and a house and a red car and you
And the paper on which you once drew a world
As a pack of cards that sequentially revealed the next

To last thing seen as an animal falls.
You stood on that ground and it was under your feet.
And then you walked away.

DEPARTURE

God's nose-end,
White nothing tower,
White-bearded, socketed face.

Fixed prison. World of grub-
White birds' litter,
Frost, love, snowflake, fat,

Iceribbed rink, moo color,
Famished ghost,
Movie-screen

And Byron's thumb-size lambs.
Behind this is: I am.
And then: I am

The magenta delving
Into death. See
My muddy blameless blood.

It skirts my blankness, as that
Insufferable mood flows before the wind.
Night's the room. Dream-filmed.

GONE

How does the river get to where it's going?
Roll the clouds over it and spare me.
I didn't want to be the myth
Of Cassandra. Looking into her doom-mirror
And telling you what she sees there.

Here's the self, she says, and here's the natural
World. Here's the ear and listen,
The cannon exploding its last blast.
The slip of a moon admonishment
To the concept of completion.

And now in spite of sorrow unending, the sky is more,
Beautiful than it's ever been.
Blue and night-blue above a string of pale April yellow
Which stands in for incandescent clarity,
Which is heard as if only.

And then not like a dropped curtain
But evening dark and darker
Until a hand is no longer a hand
And yellow goes green-yellow, then narrows to nothing.
And pace is everything. The slow effacement

Of the window through which she looks
And the mirror as far away
Now as a star and we are
Both gone. Both from each other
And from the myth we were.

APRIL IS ENDING

The commenting wolf
(My, what little sense you make, Dearie) is silent now.
Everyone agrees — sense is not something made.

Sense is the schematic diagram of idealization.
It's easy to backtrack and make day melt
Back into what it was formed from:

Grief and the mute universe.
Numbers from one to twelve
Once marked the periphery

Of a hospital clock's untiring round.
The dead of May waited for the dead of June to join them.
Once I loved you, always I'll love you.

The dull mind is a different kind
Of world. Earth was frozen.

HOW BEAUTIFUL

A personal lens: glass bending rays
That gave one that day's news
Saying each and every day,

Just remember you are standing
On a planet that's evolving.
How beautiful, she thought, what distance does

For water, the view from above or afar.
In last night's dream, they were back again
At the beginning. She was a child

And he was a child.
A plane lit down and left her there.
Cold whitening the white sky whiter.

Then a scalpel cut her open for all the world
To be a sea.

CURTAINS OF EMPTINESS

This is what he couldn't see—
The sea path, rocks smashed past vertical
From some previous TNT force.
He was done for. He was over.

Yet her mind ticked
With his still presence. How does one live
With sorrow? His hand on her shoulder
Saying, your love

Of precision will only get you in trouble.
Your sense of lack will too.
She dreamed him alive and ill.
Pietà-like. She dreamed him

At every age. Ten and less. Fourteen and taller.
The tick ticking back and forward like the sea
Crashing against the wet black rock
Of clarity and circumstance.

The skating scene seen again
And again, against the replay of a fever at four,
The day in May when he was in withdrawal
And a doctor said almost and dead.

Words from where
They watched while he ate white ice cream
With a wooden spoon. He said, My
Doesn't this taste good?

Leading everyone to believe he meant to live
Forever. Now she was sickened
By the essence of recollection.

GUILT

Would it ever go away?
Married to the inexhaustible
Need to be accurate,
Were twenty little questions like,

Is this who he was? Who
Wants to know? And she,
Because she couldn't erase herself, was left
Only with her love of precision

And her lack. Along with the sudden
Familiarity with grief. That all
Of nothing. And him, perched in her mind,
Never to be unbalanced again.

Never to be hospital bedded, mother loved.
Oh, he's peaceful now, they told her.
And she wondered
Whether they could know anything

About what they'd never been.
She was at the corner now and turning
Her back on where winter met spring.
Where two seasons

Melted into one. That year after.
Your death. His death. Her death.

SHE REMEMBERED

A cigarette lighter, a circle drawn
From a car's compartmentalized dash.
The tip of the cigarette stuck
And became a stunning ember.
She remembered a cast on a wrist,
A fracture. The buzz of a saw
Seen coming too close. A see-saw then
A casket. Then
The trail went dead. She was seven.
Her mother said to her cousin,
Who was trying to soothe her, Oh, she
Doesn't even know why she's crying.
But she did. She knew
Then and she knew now.
She looked up. She saw
The moon's faux beam touching nothing.
She remembered a bee sting. She was driving
A car and the bee flew in the window
And somehow entered a slit—a sleeve
Or the narrow divide at the neck where the collar splits—
And found itself the equivalent of miffed
And stung, not once but several times
Until she slumped over the steering wheel
And veered to the curb.
Someone came out of a café to see
If she was okay.
We thought you were having a heart attack.
And they laughed.
On a scale where dead equals all,
It was a fractional thing. A bee sting.
The odd ceremony of stopping, of holding

Her hand to her chest, the pain
That grew to a compelling drone
Until she turned the car around and went home
And put ice on her chest and rested.
She remembered a canoe. She and someone.
Was it a cousin? On a calm, crystalline surface
Until suddenly they reached the rapids.
Sometime after that the canoe tipped over.
Somehow they righted it and were back in
Again. Was it remembered? Or a dream
In which she wore red. A little Lulu comic
On the dock. Primitive flotsam
In the mind's continual muffled
Increment of tickytickytick. Time leveled
To a horizontal reverse where a boy walks back
Into a room and says, It's only a dream.

EVIDENCE

This is the wilderness
Of evidence: a tangled thought
Becomes a book
On a dresser unread,

Pages stacked in predictable sequence:
Numbers behaving as numbers do,
Promising a future and
Lining up at the door and waiting

Patiently to enter.
You become the connection
Thread to the cat that lost its tail
And subsequently invented tragedy.

That man named Mac is right
When he says a thousand voices say
Live and forget
The rest. Goodnight.

And goodbye. You
With your archangel name.
You with your teardrop beads
Lined up along the thread

Through the eye
Of the needle in the blankstack.
Every thread leads to the death
Day. I lost you. I love you.

How changed we are.
Otherwise no longer exists.
There is only stasis, continually
Granting ceremony to the moment.

WORSE

You are in the zebra crossing,
Moving into the tornado green morning,
The shabby irradiation
Of sunlight seen through the hint
Of rain about to be. Death is
A jerky reversal of forward momentum.
Back into memory. Into a cereal bowl
On a table decades ago, the color of an orange
Aspirin for a fever at age four
That produced a heat-filled forehead hallucination.
Think of a hive made of glass, all the bees,
Theoretically at least, describable but not all at once.
That's my mind and you
Are doing all the things you ever did all at once.
There are so many
Of you. Many more than several. Thirty-seven
Years of behavior. Nothing terrible
Has happened as yet except the uneven drone
Inside is an announcement that there will be something
Like a sting only much much worse.

LET'S GO BACK

To the beginning morning dawning
With the birth of all
That you would be. The chill hand
Of January teaching time to the clock.

And now July, that ladder half-
Birthday that marks nothing but a rake
That pushes back the pack
Of wild dogs into a cage.

There is no worse
Than this last act where you disappear
Behind the curtain of addiction catastrophe.
Look how simple
Action is. And now there is no more.

ONE THING

The one thing he was
Not was an object. The other thing
He was not was dead.

Dissolve changed nothing but the form.
He was what he'd always been—
Disquiet acutely attended.

Not dead. Not over.
He sat on a chair or stood in a doorway
Or stayed propped against a hospital pillow where

Fluorescent green cast its pall over white.
Now he looked out over the vast
Landscape with a silent heart's potential

To become audible. If only
It would say lubdub and be alive.
In the distance, cause for happiness couldn't be seen

While sorrow wound itself around the tree trunk.
Consequence stalked.
Demon memories put on monkey faces

And made fun behind every back.
Are you here to help me,
Or to bother me? she asked him.

He continued to both console and unnerve.
All this in the house that she thought of
As This-One-And-Only-Life.

THE ESSENCE

The world behind the mirror
Was heartrendingly beautiful
And convulsively sad.

In it, the almost-gone beloved was always turning
A corner. His back in an overcoat.
Up front, a high wind was threatening

To upend the stage
And the players with it and bring the curtain down.
The cyclone would be worth the risk,

But if only
The world would look new again.
Dumb numbers gawked from the clock face.

The hole where the hands were
Supposed to be was empty
And endless. A bell tolled erratically

And never on the hour. Punishment was meted out
As it was supposed to be, too—
Continually.

THERE IS ONLY THIS

Now, 12:31 turning over in its bed,
Its head to the feet of another, shrouded
In a body bag. A bee carcass.

I'm at the door
Of the dark watching the saddest story: the loss
Of everything

Flickers on the dream screen.
A woman dead centered
Is saying something

It takes great patience to hear. My ear is a beach
And the sea is talking to it incessantly.
It sounds like

She is saying, "My mouth is a rock,
Please roll it away."
But I doubt that I have it

Within me to do it, even if it is what she wants.

A YEAR ENDS

There were no partitions to this
But finally a year was.
Q: How does a body disappear?
A: It doesn't.

Molecules in motion
And memory, the endless M words.
He continued to live in the space that it took
To conjure him up.

A window in the brain opened
When something was ready
To be said or heard. When it closed
He stood in the corner

Of every room facing out.
Facing the air between him and her.
He lived in her mind
As a limited aspect where time kept circling

A track that went back
To the death day. It ended
With a silver-tooth trap,
The spring of which never rusted:

If she had only done X,
When instead she'd done Y.
Then he would see this
Sun, this rain, this whatever

Light bulb blink as it was
About to go out. Define a day
For me, someone said to her.
Tragic from beginning to end.

YOU WERE YOU ARE ELEGY

Fragile like a child is fragile.
Destined not to be forever.
Destined to become other
To mother. Here I am
Sitting on a chair, thinking
About you. Thinking
About how it was
To talk to you.
How sometimes it was wonderful
And sometimes it was awful.
How drugs when drugs were
Undid the good almost entirely
But not entirely
Because good could always be seen
Glimmering like lame glimmers
In the window of a shop
Called Beautiful
Things Never Last Forever.
I loved you. I love you. You were.
And you are. Life is experience.
It's all so simple. Experience is
The chair we sit on.
The sitting. The thinking
Of you where you are a blank
To be filled
In by missing. I loved you.
I love you like I love
All beautiful things.
True beauty is truly seldom.
You were. You are
In May. May now is looking onto

The June that is coming up.
This is how I measure
The year. Everything Was My Fault
Has been the theme of the song
I've been singing,
Even when you've told me to quiet.
I haven't been quiet.
I've been crying. I think you
Have forgiven me. You keep
Putting your hand on my shoulder
When I'm crying.
Thank you for that. And
For the ineffable sense
Of continuance. You were. You are
The brightest thing in the shop window
And the most beautiful seldom I ever saw.

ANARCHY

The white-smocked hands her a death-head.
A fabulous marvel of eyebaths and places
Behind the fissured, shoulder-high moon.
Yellow timbers tidy under the dawn.
The whole enough of richness and marble and stone.

He split into good-mother and ill-bred
Mother—displaced arm, pallid tooth,
Many-breasted heart—and now
She was sameness, a puppet face, a red-freckled mask.
A well heart, dissolving.

How do the stars overhead see the city?
Love is the point. Love is the little
Swaddled sinewy ear tubes, food fissures.
A handkerchief on the bare
Flimsy pink limb. Elusive eye-button mind.

ANNIVERSARY

A date came forward, a song accompanied it.
She was up. The bat cracked, but not really.
It was only sound, the pathetic desire to be heard.
Grief was complicated. Thoughts
Washed against a reef, as if metaphor
Would make it less real. Or more.
Last night's dream was the machine
That brought the day forward
Into being. In it, he was young again.

She was herself. There was a lack
Of understanding between them.
There was a suitcase. There was a sense
Of frustration that this was the way it would always be.
Awake, she no longer said, "Come back," to the absence
Now there was another refrain.
It replaced all the gone ones and replayed ad infinitum.
She didn't know how to go on from here.
She was tired of the old foot-forward pattern,

A bite of bread, a bit of butter. Would she forget
If she could? Yes. But did she forget? No.
By now, she thought, the terrain should be routine.
But it wasn't. It was instead
A world of her own. Alone. With comma moths
Embarking one after the other
In an inner still life landscape.
Where the brushwork wasn't the stuff of dreams
But real and infinitely mutable.

VISITING

The city's dirty edges are found and are
Unsoftened, unchanged.
Also the charcoal windows

That look onto the low lit ceiling
Of night. You whose name is you
Are a fantasy that remains

After I wake from a dream of walking
Shoeless in snow. Cold is that cold.
Look at all the meaningless gestures

People keep
Making: flowers in a vase and overheard
Overblown terms like seldom

And massive, and missive and all
The words except
I miss you. For me meaning is pared

Down to forever. We loved this:
Dark city and its boxy art
Of living. Goodnight. I will see you

Tomorrow. I know I will.
But no more speaking
Out loud. Only the excavation

And finding the old. The no longer
Attached you and me.
Your ragged crown

Of good is a trinket buried
In curb debris.
Rust of Prince unheralded.

Rust of all we were when all was good.
Goodnight. The ordeal comes
To its periodic end

Which simply means
The ahead is again.

ACKNOWLEDGMENTS

Thanks to Fanny Howe for choosing poems from *Elegy* for the Poetry Society of America's 2005 Alice Fay di Castagnola Award for a manuscript-in-progress. And more thanks to the Guggenheim Foundation for a grant that provided the time to write, and to the Bogliasco Foundation for a fellowship at the Liguria Study Center, where some of these poems were written.

And to the editors of the following publications in which versions of these poems first appeared:

Boston Review: "The Essence" and "Worse"; *Call: A Review:* "Beneath the Din," "A Sonata for Four Hands, II" "September Is," "The Watch," "Anarchy," and "Once"; *Columbia Magazine:* "No More," "Let's Go Back," "Gone," "January Elegy," "She Remembered," and "November Elegy"; *Cordite.com* (Australia): "In Order Means Neat and Not Next" and "Definitely"; *Crowd:* "Enclosure," "February Elegy," and "She Said"; *Jacket.com* (Australia): "Intractable, and Irreversible," "Where Once," and "How Beautiful"; *Jubilat:* "To Ash" and "Goodbye Is Another Word for Not"; *Laurel Review:* "Words," "What If," and "A Boy at Play Is an Actor in a Tragedy"; *Luna:* "The Game" and "A Sonata for Four Hands"; *The New Yorker:* "Landscape with the Fall of Icarus"; *No: A Journal of the Arts:* "Utopian Longing Becomes More Absurd" and "We Are Only Human"; *Notre Dame Review:* "Curtains of Emptiness" and "No Exit"; *The Paris Review:* "The Cruel Wheel Turns Twice," "Historical Landscape," "Departure," "What Is So Frightening," and "Ode to History"; *Pleiades:* "Talk to Me," "She Remembers His Hat," "Tragedy," "There Is No Pretending," "Now," and "The Role of Elegy"; *Poetry:* "You Were

You Are Elegy"; *Provincetown Arts:* "Evidence"; *Prairie Schooner:* "Hell" and "Untitled"; *Runes:* "Where"; *Verse:* "The Opening"; *The Yale Review:* "Don't"

Thanks to Heather McHugh for selecting the poem "The Opening" for inclusion in *The Best American Poetry* (series ed. David Lehman, Scribner 2007), and to Michael Theune for including "The Game" in *Structure & Surprise* (Teachers and Writers Collaborative 2007). "Anarchy" was printed as a broadside by the Spring 2007 Book Arts class at New Mexico State University.

To Gary Bang, a lifetime of gratitude. And to friends and family, the same.

"A Sonata for Four Hands, II" is for Robert Marvin Garcia Hunt.
"September Is" is for Caitlin Corrigan.
"Goodbye Is Another Word for Not" is for Dory Morris.
"The Watch" is for Norine Carroll.
"Heartbreaking" is for David Miller and Kelly Loftus.

A million thanks to Scott Merritt.

MARY JO BANG is the author of four previous poetry collections: *The Eye Like a Strange Balloon, Louise in Love, The Downstream Extremity of the Isle of Swans,* and *Apology for Want.* She has received a fellowship from the Guggenheim Foundation, a Hodder Fellowship from Princeton University, and has twice won the Alice Fay di Castagnola Award from the Poetry Society of America. She lives in Saint Louis, Missouri, where she is a professor of English and director of the creative writing program at Washington University.

The text of *Elegy* has been set in Century Schoolbook, a font cut by Monotype in 1934, and based on Century Expanded, designed by Linn Boyd Benton in 1894.

Book design by Wendy Holdman. Composition by Prism Publishing Center. Manufactured by Bang Printing on acid-free paper.